D1238931

Note to Parents and Teachers

The SCIENCE STARTERS series introduces key science vocabulary to young children while encouraging them to discover and understand the world around them. The series works as a set of graded readers in three levels.

LEVEL 1: BEGINNING TO READ
These books can be read alone or as part of guided or group reading.
Each book has three sections:

• Information pages that introduce new words. These key words appear in bold throughout the book for easy recognition.
• A lively story that recalls this vocabulary and encourages children to use these words when they talk and write.
• A quiz and word search ask children to look back and recall what they have read.

DIGGERS AND TOOLS AT WORK looks at MACHINES. Below are some answers related to the questions on the information spreads that parents, carers, and teachers can use to discuss and develop further ideas and concepts:

p. 5 *What other jobs can machines do?* Encourage children to think about machines in groups, e.g. machines that clean (washing machine, roadsweeper), carry us (cars, buses, and trains), help us keep in touch (e.g. telephones), or entertain us (TVs, radios, toys).

p. 7 *What other fast machines can you think of?* You could group these by land, sea, and air, e.g. cars, ambulances; speedboats and hovercraft; airplanes and helicopters.

p. 9 *Why should you be careful with sharp tools?* Remind children not to touch knives, saws, chisels, and other sharp tools and to be very careful when handling scissors.

p. 11 *What other machines have wheels?* Point out that as well as machines that roll along, from tractors and cars to shopping carts and skateboards, objects such as doorknobs, merry-go-rounds, and ferris wheels also spin like a wheel.

p. 13 *What does an engine need to give it energy?* Engines need fuel to give them energy. The motor in an electric machine needs electricity from a socket or a battery.

p. 17 *Why does a train need a very strong engine?* Reinforce the idea that big machines need more power, e.g. a jumbo jet has much more powerful engines than a small airplane.

p. 19 *How do you dig a hole? Are you as fast as a digger?* You can dig a big hole with a shovel, but a powerful engine helps a machine dig much faster.

p. 21 *What boats move on water without an engine?* Sailing boats and windsurfers are pushed along by the wind. You move rowing boats or canoes using oars and paddles.

ADVISORY TEAM

Educational Consultant
Andrea Bright—Science Coordinator, Trafalgar Junior School

Literacy Consultant
Jackie Holderness—former Principal Lecturer in Primary Education, Westminster Institute, Oxford Brookes University

Series Consultants
Anne Fussell—Early Years Teacher and University Tutor, Westminster Institute, Oxford Brookes University

David Fussell—C.Chem., FRSC

CONTENTS

© Aladdin Books Ltd 2007

Designed and produced by
Aladdin Books Ltd

First published in
the United States in 2007 by
Stargazer Books
c/o The Creative Company
123 South Broad Street
P.O. Box 227
Mankato, Minnesota 56002

Printed in the United States
All rights reserved

Editor: Sally Hewitt
Design: Flick, Book Design
and Graphics
Picture Research:
Alexa Brown

Thanks to:
• The pupils of Trafalgar Infants School
for appearing as models in this book.
• Debbie Staynes for helping to organize
the photoshoots, and the pupils and
teachers of Trafalgar Junior School and
St. Nicholas C.E. Infant School for
testing the sample books.

**Library of Congress Cataloging-in-
Publication Data**

Pipe, Jim, 1966-
    Machines / by Jim Pipe.
        p. cm. -- (Science starters. Level 1)
    Includes index.
    ISBN 978-1-59604-078-6
    1. Machinery--Juvenile literature.
    I. Title. II. Series.

TJ147.P56 2006
621.8--dc22

2005056016

Photocredits:
*l-left, r-right, b-bottom, t-top,
c-center, m-middle*
Front cover tl, 8t, 32mlt — USDA.
Front cover tm, 7 both, 20t, 32mrb
— Scania. Front cover tr, 2tl, 9, 10,
12b, 31ml, 32mrt — US Navy.
Front cover b, 3, 5t, 11t, 13, 18,
22tr, 31br, 32ml, 32br — John
Deere. 2ml, 4b, 11br, 31tr, 32tl —
Renault. 2bl, 20br, 23tr, 32mlb &
bl — Digital Vision. 4tr, 6b, 16br,
17, 19, 22b, 26ml, 28ml, 29t, 31mr,
32tr — Corbis. 6b, 12tr — TongRo.
6tr, 15ml — Ingram Publishing.
8br, 15tr, 24-25 all, 28bl, 30tl —
Marc Arundale / Select Publishing.
14bl, 15br, 26tr, 30mr, 32mr —
Jim Pipe. 14br — Comstock. 16t —
Digital Vision. 21 — NASA. 23b,
29b — PBD. 27t — Select Pictures.
27br — Photodisc. 28tl — Corel.

416 4070

MACHINES

Diggers and Tools at Work

by Jim Pipe

Stargazer Books

Everywhere you go, **machines** are at **work**.

Cars and trucks help us to move about.

Tractors **work** on a farm.

Diggers **work** on the roads.

Some **machines** are just for fun!

• What other jobs can machines do?

How do machines help us?

Tools help us to
do small jobs.

A big truck is very **strong**.
It can do heavy jobs.

6

A bus goes **fast**. It can take us a long way.

A fire engine comes **fast** to keep us safe.

• What other fast machines can you think of?

Tools help us
to make things.

Scissors

We **hit** a nail with a hammer.
We **cut** paper with scissors.

We push and pull a saw to **cut** wood.

Many **tools** are sharp.
They are made from metal.

• *Why should you be careful with sharp tools?*

Bicycle

Many machines have **wheels.**

Wheels make it easy to move.
They **roll** along the ground.

10

Track

Wheels and tracks can **roll** over bumpy ground.

A driver **turns** a **wheel** to go left or right.

• What other machines have wheels?

Some machines have no **engine**.

We push the pedals to make a bicycle move.

We push a wheelbarrow.

Many machines have an **engine**.

The **engine** pushes and pulls.
It makes the wheels go around.

Engine

• What does an engine need to give it energy?

Electric machines do jobs at home.
Motors make them push and pull.

Electric machines clean floors.
They also wash clothes and dishes.

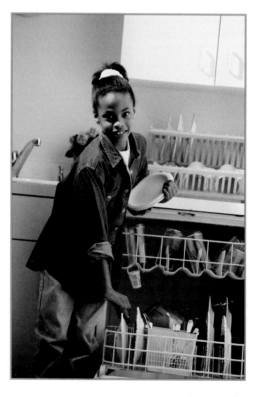

Vacuum cleaner   **Dishwasher**

14

A **motor** helps
a CD player
play music.

A **motor** makes
the hands on
an **electric**
clock move.

A **motor** makes an
electric toy move.

• What other machines and tools do jobs at home?

Machines with engines and wheels **carry** us about.
A car can **carry** a whole family.

A bus can **carry** a whole class.

16

A train pulls lots of passenger cars.
It can **carry** a whole school!

A train has lots of wheels.
Its strong engine has a lot of **power**.

• Why does a train need a very strong engine?

Some machines are made for hard work.

A digger uses tools to **dig** and carry.
Wheels and tracks help it move.
Its strong engine has lots of power.

Digger

Diggers, trucks, and cranes
help us **build** roads and houses.

What is this crane trying to **lift**?

Crane

• How do you dig a hole? Are you as fast as a digger?

Machines can move
on land, sea, and air.

A boat **floats**
on water.

An airplane can **fly**
in the air.

A rocket can **fly** into space!

• What boats move on water without an engine?

Big machines
need a **driver**.

A **driver controls**
a digger.

A pilot **controls** an airplane.

You can **control** machines, too.

You pull a rope to steer a go-kart.

You push a button to switch on an electric machine.

Television

• What machine would you like to drive?

NOISY MACHINE!

Read the story and look for words about **machines**.

Dad is using his **electric power tool.**

It **works fast,**
but it is very noisy!

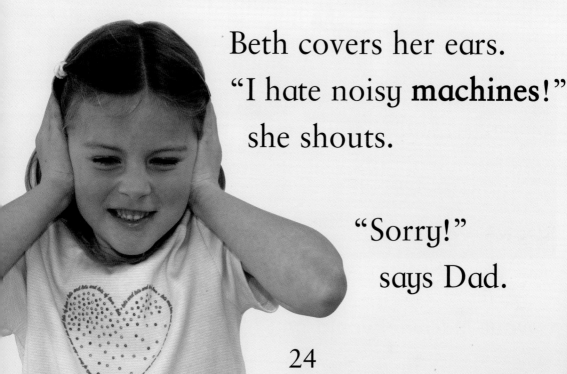

Beth covers her ears.
"I hate noisy **machines!**"
she shouts.

"Sorry!"
says Dad.

24

Dan doesn't mind.

He likes **electric** toys
with noisy **motors.**

He loves to watch
big diggers at **work.**

"Let's go to the park.
It will be quiet
there," says Dad.

"The washing
machine can
clean my smelly
socks while we
are out!"

On the way, a big
bus drives past.

"Smelly **machine!**"
says Beth.

Dan waves
at the **driver**.
He likes **machines**
with **wheels**.

He'd love to ride
a **fast** motorcycle!

"Look over there, Dan," says Dad.
"What are those **machines building?**"

Diggers are **digging** a big hole.
A crane is **lifting** a heavy load.
"Noisy **machines!**" says Beth. "Let's go!"

At the park, skaters **roll** along the path.

"Are skates
machines?" asks Dan.
"Yes," says Beth.
"They have **wheels.**"

A sailboat is **floating** on the lake.

It has no **engine**. "At last, a quiet **machine!**" says Beth.

Dan sees some kites. "They **fly** without an **engine**," he says.

"You **control** a kite by pulling on the string," says Dad.

A big airplane **flies** by.
"Noisy **machine!**" shouts Beth.

They walk to the playground.
"You'll like these **machines**, Beth!"
laughs Dad.

They play on the
carousel. It spins
like a **wheel**.

29

Dan and Beth **carry** food home for dinner. Dad **cuts** up the food with a knife.

Beth switches on her CD player. Dad covers his ears. "Noisy **machine!**" he laughs.

Look around your home or school. What jobs are **machines** doing?

Draw a picture of a **machine**. Write a label to say what it is.

Car

QUIZ

What **machines work** on a farm?

Answer on page 4

What are sharp **tools** made of?

Answer on page 9

Can a train **carry** more than a car?

Answer on page 17

Who **controls** a digger?

Answer on page 22

Did you know the answers? Give yourself a

Do you remember these words about **machines**?
Well done! Can you remember any more?

 **work** page 4

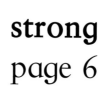 **strong** page 6

 **tool** page 8

wheel page 10

 **engine** page 13

motor page 15

 **carry** page 16

float page 20

 **fly** page 20

driver page 22